# Joke Book

First published 2011 by Macmillan Children's Books
a division of Macmillan Publishers Limited
20 New Wharf Road, London N1 9RR
Basingstoke and Oxford
Associated companies throughout the world
www.panmacmillan.com

ISBN 978-1-4472-0003-1

1 3 5 7 9 8 6 4 2

A CIP catalogue record for this book is available from
the British Library.

Typeset by Gary Knight
Printed and bound by CPI Group (UK) Ltd, Croydon CRO 4YY

# Joke Book

MACMILLAN CHILDREN'S BOOKS

What did the Bin Weevil
say when his friend
turned up an hour late?

Where have you
Bin, Weevil?

What did the Nest Inspector study at school?
Bin-terior design.

What did the firefly
say to her best friend?
You glow girl!

What did the big sister bug
say to her younger brother?
**Stop bugging me.**

What did one flea say to the other flea
when they came out of the movies?
**Should we walk, or take the dog?**

Bin Weevil: Mum, can we go to
France this year?
**Bin Weevil Mum: No dear, we're
going to grease.**

# Where can you find the biggest spider?
## The world wide web.

# What do you call a baby ant?
## An inf-ant.

# What do you get if you cross a Weevil with a bin?
## A Bin Weevil.

Which bug is not allowed
in the boys' toilets?
**The ladybug.**

What did the Bin Weevil
check before boarding the plane?
**His buggage.**

Which insect came to help out at school?
**The insect-retary.**

Why was the bee's
hair sticky?
Because she used a
honey-comb.

Why didn't the butterflies look at the website?
Their parents warned them to avoid the net.

What happened when the dog
went to the flea circus?
He stole the show.

What do you call a Bin Weevil with no eyes?
A Bn Weevl.

How can a flea learn to use a computer?
He has to start from scratch.

What does a caterpillar do on
the first of January?
Turns over a new leaf.

What do a spider and a duck
have in common?
They both have webbed feet.

Where would you put an injured insect?
In an antbulance.

What do you call a
nervous Bin Weevil?
A jitterbug.

What do you call a Bin Pet with no legs?
Anything you like, it still won't come to you.

What do moths study at school?
Mothmatics.

What do you call singing insects?
Humbugs.

**Why was the ant confused?**
Because his uncles were ants.

**Why was the Egyptian bug confused?**
Because its daddy was a mummy.

What did Fling say to the mushroom?
You're a fun-gi.

How do you make
a moth ball?
Hit him with a
fly swatter.

Why did the Bin Weevil climb on to the cafe roof?
Because the sign said 'Drinks are on the house'.

What kind of bee gets
into lots of fights?
**A rumble bee.**

What do you call an
old Bin Weevil?
**A has-bin.**

What type of food can you
find in a bin?
**Junk food.**

# What do baby Bin Weevils travel around in?
## Buggies.

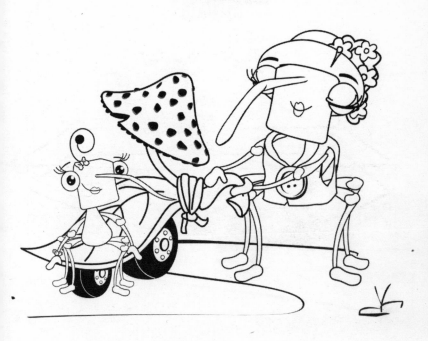

# What do apples and bogeys have in common?
## They both get picked and eaten.

# What happens when two snails have a fight?
## They slug it out.

What insect runs away
from everything?
**A flea.**

What did the Bin Weevil DJ say?
**Let's buggie!**

What's the best job for a spider?
**A website-builder.**

Two fleas were running across the top of a cereal packet. 'Why are we running so fast?' said one. The other replied, 'Because it says "tear along the dotted line!"'

What did the Bin Weevil say to the bin?
You're rubbish.

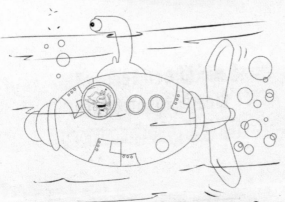

What can fly underwater?
A wasp in a submarine.

What did the slug
say as he fell off
the branch?
**How slime flies.**

How do you keep a Bin
Weevil in suspense?
**I'll tell you tomorrow.**

What is a wasp's favourite city?
**Stingapore.**

What do you call a Bin Weevil with headphones on?
Anything you like, she can't hear you!

What's the biggest moth in the world?
A mammoth.

What do you call a cheerful flea?
A hoptimist.

**What has wheels and flies?**
**A wheelie bin.**

**What do you call two spiders**
**who have just got married?**
**Newly-webs.**

**How do fireflies start a race?**
**Ready, steady, glow!**

What lies on its back 100 feet in the air?
An upside-down centipede.

What did the big Weevil say to the little Weevil?
You're the lesser of two Weevils.

When does a bee
fly with its legs
crossed?
When it's looking
for a BP station.

# Why did the bin throw up?
## Because it was too full.

# What do you call a Bin Weevil on wheels?
## A buggy.

# What does an earwig say when
# it falls off a wall?
## 'Ere we go.

Why was lightning coming from Lab's Lab?
**He was brainstorming.**

$x = (y+3)/v$

A Bin Weevil walks into Tum's Diner and begins climbing across the ceiling and down the walls. He stops, climbs down to the floor and orders a Bin Burger.

'That was unusual,' says one waitress after he left.

'I know,' agrees another waitress, 'he usually orders the double Bin Burger.'

What do you call a Bin Weevil with a cold?
**A Bin Sneezil.**

AchoO!

What did the Nest Inspector say when
visiting the ant's nest?
**This is brilli-ant.**

What has fifty legs but can't walk?
**Half a centipede.**

What's worse than taking a bite out of your sandwich and finding a Bin Weevil?
**Finding half a Bin Weevil.**

How does a flea get from place to place?
**By itch-hiking.**

What's a grasshopper? **An insect on a pogo stick.**

Which sport are Bin Weevils scared to play?
Squash.

One Bin Weevil asked her friend, 'Why can't
our antennae be twelve inches long?'
Her friend replied,
'Because then they would be a foot.'

What did the firefly say
before it left the party?
Goodbye, I'll be glowing now.

Why were two Bin Weevils playing
football on a saucer?
They were practising for the cup.

What did the daddy bin say to the baby bin?
Stop talking trash!

Doctor, Doctor, I keep seeing insects everywhere!
Yes I know, there's a bug going round.

How do snails get their shells so shiny?
They use snail varnish.

What do you get
when you cross a
Bin Weevil with a
rabbit?
Bugs Bunny.

What happened to the glow-worm
when he was squashed?
He was de-lighted.

# What's the best advice to give to a worm?
## Sleep late!

# What is Flem's favourite holiday destination?
## Snotland.

# What do you call an ant with five pairs of eyes?
## Antteneye.

# What is a snail?
## A slug wearing a crash helmet.

Two Bin Weevils were munching on some
rubbish in an alley, when one started a
discussion about a new restaurant.
'I was in this new restaurant across the street,'
he said. 'It's so clean! The kitchen is spotless,
and the floors are gleaming. There isn't a speck
of dirt anywhere – the whole place shines.'
'Please,' said the other Bin Weevil, frowning.
**Not while I'm eating!**

What kind of bug is good at maths?
**An account-ant.**

How many insects are needed to fill
an apartment block?
**Ten-ants.**

Why did the Bin Weevil cross the road?
**To bug the chicken.**

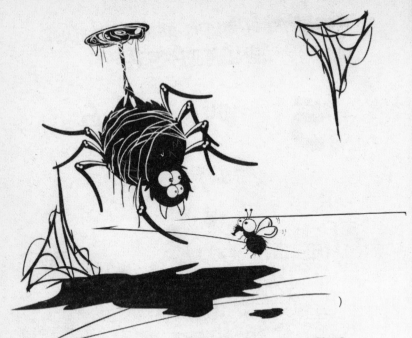

How does a spider greet a fly?
Pleased to eat you.

What do you call a
bee whose buzz you
can't quite hear?
A mumble bee.

Why did the spider buy a car?
So he could take it out for a spin.

What do you call an ant
who can't play the piano?
**Discord-ant.**

What did the mummy bee say
to the naughty little bee?
**Bee-hive yourself.**

What do Bin Weevils say before they go to sleep?
**Don't let the bin bugs bite.**

Why do bees hum?
Because they don't know the words.

Huumm...

Why did the Bin Weevil eat his homework?
Because the teacher told him
it was a piece of cake.

What do you call crazy fleas?
Loony ticks.

**Which bee never shows off?**
**A humble bee.**

**Why did the firefly keep stealing things?**
**He was light-fingered.**

**What song did the Bin Weevil band perform?**
**Wee-vil, wee-vil rock you!**

What did one caterpillar say to the other
when a butterfly fluttered past?
You'll never get me up in one of those things.

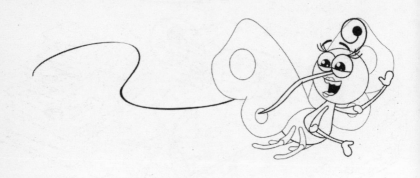

What bee is excellent for your health?
Vitamin bee.

A Bin Weevil walked into a shop,
and do you know what he said?
Ouch!

What did the bookworm say to the librarian?
**May I burrow this book?**

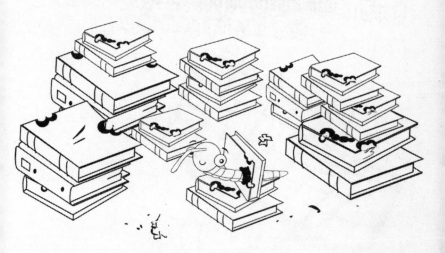

What time is it when
a fly and a flea pass
each other?
**Fly past flea.**

What do you do with a bee in winter?
**Try to swarm it up.**

What has a purple body,
ten hairy legs and eyes on stalks?
I don't know, but there's one
crawling up your leg!

What do bees chew?
Buzzle gum.

What do you call a nosy bee?
A buzzy body.

What insect talks about you behind your back?
**A cattypillar.**

pshh pshh pshh
pshh pshh pshh

Ahahaha!!!

Who wrote the book 'Insect Bites'?
**Amos Quito.**

Doctor, Doctor, I feel like a wasp.
**Buzz off!**

What do you get if you cross a bee
with a slice of beef?
**A humburger.**

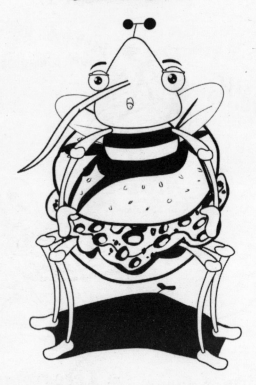

What is a Bin Weevil's favourite type of curry?
**Bin-daloo.**

How can you tell which spiders
are the trendiest?
**They have their own websites.**

What made the centipede
late for his football match?
**Putting his boots on.**

What do you call a bee who
has had a spell put on him?
**Bee-witched.**

Why are Bin Weevils nervous on Wednesdays?
**Because the bin men come on Wednesdays.**

Waiter, Waiter,
there's a fly in my soup!
Well, throw it a pea and it can play water polo.

Waiter, there's another
fly in my soup!
Don't worry, the spider on
the roll will eat it.

Waiter, Waiter,
what is this fly doing on my ice cream?
Learning to ski, Sir.

# What do you call an indecisive bee?
## A maybee.

# Where do fleas go in winter?
## Search me.

# What did the wasp say to his friend?
## I must fly now, but I'll give you a buzz later.

# What did Slam say after the pirate party?
## That was off the hook!

# Do you want to hear the joke about the bin?
## Nah, it's rubbish.

# What goes 'hum choo, hum choo'?
## A bee with a cold.

# What did the bee say to the flower?

Hello, honey.

# What did the worm journalist work for?
## An underground newspaper.

# How do you get rid of termites?
## Ex-terminite them.

How does the Queen Bee get around the hive?
She's throne.

When does a flying bug
know it's successful?
When it brings someone to their sneeze.

How do Bin Weevils like their eggs?
Rotten.

How do you tell which end of a worm is its head?
Tickle the middle and see which end laughs.

Why did the mosquito
go to the dentist?
To improve his bite.

What sport do drones play?
Beesball.

Why couldn't the butterfly
go to the dance?
It was a moth ball.

How do you start an insect race?
One, two, flea, go!

What lives in gum trees?
Stick insects.

How do we know insects are intelligent?
They always work out
where we're going to have our picnics.

Why did the moth nibble the carpet?
He wanted to see the floor show.

Why are mosquitoes annoying?
Because they get under your skin.

# What's an insect's best chat-up line?

**Hello, is this stool taken?**

# What do fireflies eat?
**Light meals.**

# What kind of bugs live in clocks?
**Ticks.**

How do you make a butterfly?
Flick it out of the
butter dish with a knife.

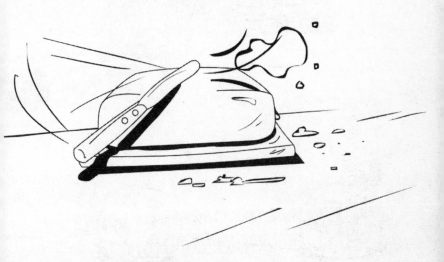

Why was the moth so annoying?
He kept picking
holes in everything.

Why was the bug
kicked out of the park?
It was a litterbug.

**What does a spider do when he gets angry?**
**He goes up the wall.**

**Why was the glow-worm upset?**
**Because she didn't know if she was coming or glowing.**

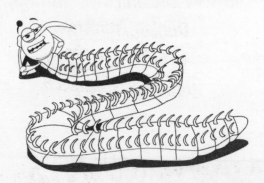

**What does millennium mean?**
**It's an insect with an awful lot of legs.**

What did the maggot say to his friend
who was stuck in an apple?
**Worm your way out of that one!**

Doctor, Doctor,
I feel like a bin.
**Don't talk rubbish!**

What's even better than a talking dog?
**A spelling bee.**

# Why was the glow-worm unhappy?
## Because her children weren't that bright.

Knock, knock!
Who's there?
Weevil.
Weevil who?
Weevil work it out.

Knock, knock!
Who's there?
Beezer.
Beezer who?
Beezer black and yellow.

# Where's the best place to buy bugs?
## A flea market.

# Where do you take a sick wasp?
## To waspital.

# What is a Bin Weevil's favourite game?
## Bin-go.

**What is a Bin Weevil's favourite sport?**
**Cricket.**

**Why did the flea fail his exams?**
**He wasn't up to scratch.**

plonk

**What goes '99, plonk, 99, plonk, 99, plonk'?**
**A centipede with a wooden leg.**

A woman kept going to the shop
to buy mothballs.
'You must have lots of moths,'
said the shop assistant.
'I have,' agreed the woman.
'And I spend all day throwing mothballs at
them, but I never seem to hit any.'

What is a Bin Weevil's favourite car?
A beetle.

What do you call a fly with no wings?
A walk.

What happened to the bedbugs who fell in love?
They got married in the spring.

What did the boy centipede say
to the girl centipede?
I want to hold your hand, hand, hand...

Why did the Queen Bee
kick out all the other bees?
Because they kept
droning on and on.

What's the biggest ant
in the world?
An eleph-ant

What would you
give a sick ant?
Ant-ibiotics.

How do bees
make money?
They cell their honey.

Why was the Bin Weevil sad?
Because he was down in the dumps.

What's a snail's favourite
summertime toy?
Slip and slide.

What's the definition of a caterpillar?
A worm wearing a fur coat.

**How can you keep flies out of the kitchen?**
**Put a bucket of manure in the living room.**

**How do insects communicate with each other?**
**By bee mail.**

**What happens when a flea gets angry?**
**It gets hopping mad.**

What did the boy maggot say
to the girl maggot?
What's a nice girl like you doing in
a joint like this?

What goes 'ha ha ha BONK'?
A Bin Weevil laughing its head off.

What kind of bee drops things?
A fumble bee.

# What do you call a slug?
## A homeless snail.

# How do bees travel?
## They take the buzz.

# Why did the fly fly?
## Because the spider spied her.

CONTRIBUTORS

Bin Weevils and Macmillan Children's Books would like to thank the following
Bin Weevils for submitting their favourite jokes:   T = top   M = middle   B = bottom

Page 4:
T: Meevle, PHOE-
   BETHEVIKING,
   wiggy88
M: Madhatter36
B: Blossomzx

Page 5
T: Scrap7890,
   Bluebut784,
   DONNANO-
   BELE, delw,
   Ultimate-Raider,
   goldmine2
M: xxfit-kirstxx
B: goldmine2

Page 6
T: sweetrecs
M: Red49
B: sweetrecs

Page 7
T: PrImE-tImE,
   Blossomzx
M: delw, moga321
B: Durt550,
   Scrap7890

Page 8
T: sweetrecs, I
   love Cyprus

Page 9
T: Blossomzx,
   quiddy, pinky84

Page 10
T: Scrap7890
B: giantcookies

Page 11
T: squareveevil
M: Bimbles

Page 12
T: Ultimate-Raider
B: juliefirth

Page 13
T: jennalochrie
B: bugsy952

Page 14
T: I love Cyprus
M: smashrash
B: superking006

Page 15
T: cheesybums,
   ClaudiaDavies,
   markymark-
   mark
M: FAMOUS-BLUE

Page 16
T: ayacute7
M: White-xX

Page 17
T: ENZI
M: Rockmaster

Page 18
M: pinky8920

Page 19
T: nerfy
M: VertiX
B: VertiX

Page 20
T: blossomzx
B: blossomzx

Page 21
T: love-lots
M: jpagel

Page 22
M: lolli92

Page 23
T: nicekindboy79
B: princess sugar

Page 24
T: cjsmall1,
   xXxCUCIxXx
M: felix3663

Page 25
T: findnigleday-
   man
M: xxfit-kirstxx

Page 26
T: iiNicooXD
M: hedgehog-holly
B: i love Cyprus

Page 27
T: sammycatherall
M: blazer222
B: divafun-s

Page 28
T: VertiX
M: gracelize
B: VertiX

Page 29
T: VertiX
M: bugsy346

Page 30
T: MonsterMash-
   er10
B: annis2

Page 31
B: baby_hay-
   ley_xx
misslonnose

Page 34
M: crash128

Page 35
B: daffydilly

Page 36
B: rmeidl

Page 40
M: Gracemae

Page 41
B: meg098

Page 44
T: quen2
M: Ga-wai,
   dude45452

Page 46
B: floppywet123

Page 53
M: Aleema2005

Page 55
B: goldmine2

Page 56
T: silea,
   blossomzx
M: xxfit-kirstxx

Page 57
M: SQUAREGUY
B: Blossomzx

Page 60
T: chemicals10

Page 62
M: katsuma1616

Page 63
M: sweetrecs,
   roxana2
B: rosy6003

64